BBC earth

DO YOU KNOW?

Level 2

CORAL REEFS

Inspired by BBC Earth TV series and developed with input from BBC Earth natural history specialists

Written by Ruth A. Musgrave
Text adapted by Rachel Godfrey
Series Editor: Nick Coates

LADYBIRD BOOKS

UK | USA | Canada | Ireland | Australia
India | New Zealand | South Africa

Ladybird Books is part of the Penguin Random House group of companies
whose addresses can be found at global.penguinrandomhouse.com.
www.penguin.co.uk   www.puffin.co.uk   www.ladybird.co.uk

First published 2020
001

Printed in China

A CIP catalogue record for this book is available from the British Library

ISBN: 978-0-241-38281-3

All correspondence to:
Ladybird Books Ltd
Penguin Random House Children's
One Embassy Gardens, New Union Square
5 Nine Elms Lane, London SW8 5DA

Contents

New words

antenna
(antennae)

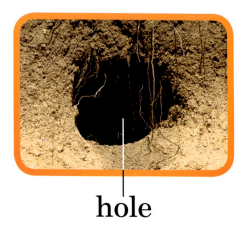

hole

plastic rubbish

recycle

rock

sand

shallow

space

sunlight

tentacle

What is a coral?

A coral is not a flower.

It is a very small animal.

A coral has **tentacles**. It catches small animals with its tentacles.

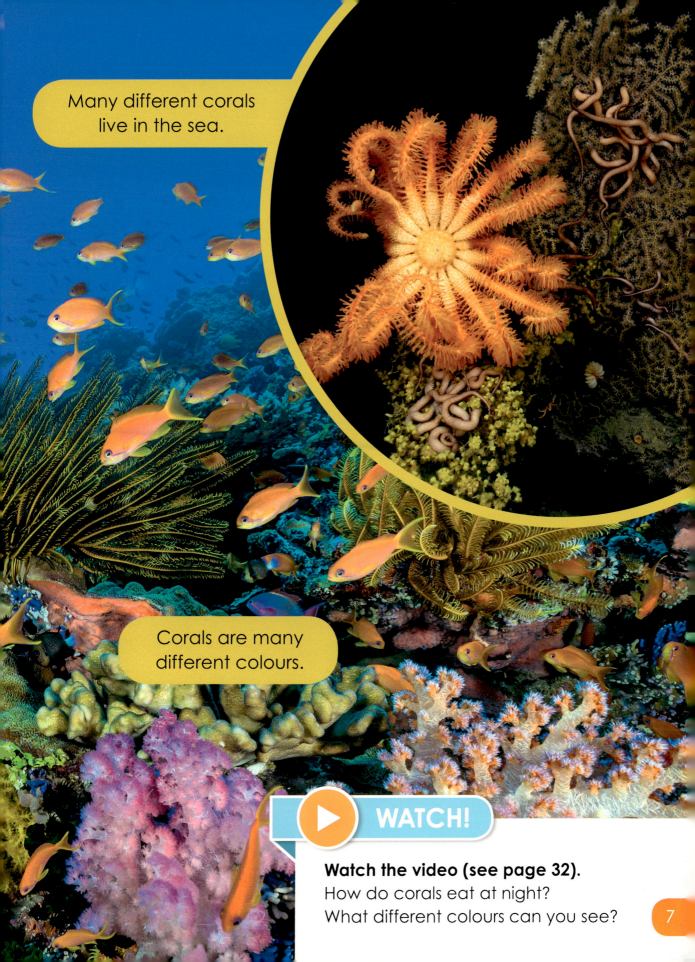

Many different corals live in the sea.

Corals are many different colours.

WATCH!

Watch the video (see page 32).
How do corals eat at night?
What different colours can you see?

What makes a coral reef?

Some reefs are small.
Some are very big.

You can see some really big reefs from **space**.

reef

Corals make their homes on **rocks**. Many corals make their homes together. This makes a coral reef.

Many animals can stay safe on the reef.

This is the Great Barrier Reef in Australia. It is a very big reef.

LOOK!

Look at the pages.
What is the name of the very big reef?

Where are coral reefs?

There are coral reefs in many different places on Earth.

Most reefs are in warm parts of the sea.

Corals need **sunlight**.

Coral reefs need **shallow** water.

There aren't any reefs in rivers. Reefs need clean seawater.

PROJECT

Work in a group.
Use books or the internet to find out where some coral reefs grow. Do you live near any reefs?

What lives near a coral reef?

Many animals live, eat and sleep on a coral reef.

Big fish eat little fish!

Hungry sharks swim near the reef.

There is a seahorse in the coral. Can you see it?

Some animals live in **holes** in the coral.

THINK!

A seahorse looks like coral.
How does that help the seahorse?

HOW does colour help cuttlefish?

Some big animals want to eat the cuttlefish!

But sometimes big animals can't see the cuttlefish, because the cuttlefish can change its colour.

A cuttlefish changes colour to catch food, too.

This crab stops because it sees different colours on the cuttlefish.

The cuttlefish catches the crab and eats it.

FIND OUT!

Use books or the internet to find out about other animals that can change colour.

What plays on the reef?

Dolphins swim together on the reef.
Sometimes they stop and play.

Young dolphins learn to catch
food by playing with the coral.

One dolphin finds some coral. It takes the coral in its mouth. It isn't easy!

The other dolphins watch. All the dolphins play with the coral.

coral

PROJECT

Work in a group.

How fast do things sink? Fill a container with water. Find things of different shapes, sizes and materials. Find out which things sink or float. Which thing sinks the fastest?

HOW do rays eat?

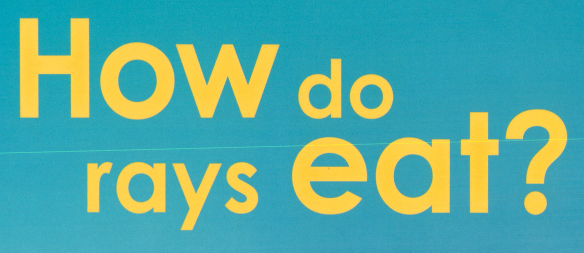

Rays sometimes go to coral reefs.

Rays are very big, but they eat very small plants and animals.

The ray swims with its mouth open. Water and food go into the ray's mouth.

This part of the ray's body catches the food.

The water comes out of the ray's body here.

THINK!

How does this ray catch its food?
Why is this a good way for the ray to eat?

How do sea turtles clean their shells?

Sometimes small plants and animals live on sea turtles' shells. This can be bad for the sea turtles.

Fish on the reef can help the sea turtles.

The sea turtles go to the reef.

The sea turtles must wait for the fish. They do not like waiting!

Fish eat the small animals and plants on the sea turtles. The sea turtles enjoy it.

▶ WATCH!

Watch the video (see page 32).
How many sea turtles are waiting to be cleaned?

What is under the sand?

A bobbit worm is under the **sand**. It is very long.

It has five **antennae**. It has big teeth.

The bobbit worm waits under the sand. But its antennae are above the sand.

A fish swims past the bobbit worm's antennae.

The bobbit worm jumps out and catches the fish.

It eats the fish under the sand.

LOOK!

Look at the pages.
How many antennae does a bobbit worm have?
Where does the bobbit worm eat the fish?

How do reef animals work together?

Some fish and octopuses catch food together.

The grouper fish and the octopus want to catch small fish.

The grouper fish cannot get the small fish, because the small fish are inside the coral.

The grouper fish shows the octopus the small fish.

The octopus puts its long arms inside the coral. The small fish come out.

Then, the grouper fish and the octopus eat the small fish.

WATCH!

Watch the video (see page 32).
How does the grouper fish show the octopus where the small fish are?

HOW does coral help fish?

This fish finds a clam. It wants to eat the meat inside.

How can the fish open the clam?

clam

The fish carries the clam to some coral.

The fish hits the clam on the coral many times.

The fish opens the clam. Now, the fish can eat the meat.

LOOK!

Look at the pages.
How does the fish carry the clam?

Why do we need coral reefs?

Coral reefs are good for the sea. They are good for the Earth.

Animals found on a reef are food for sea animals and for us, too.

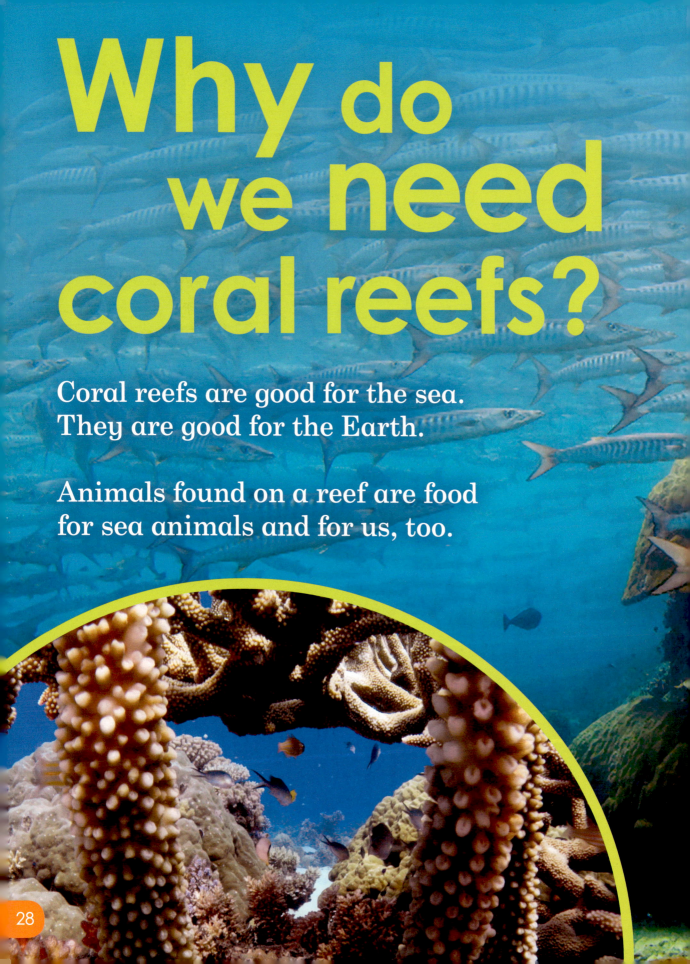

Coral and sea animals can die because there is **plastic rubbish** on the reefs.

Plastic rubbish must not go into the sea. We must **recycle** rubbish. Together, we can help the coral reefs.

PROJECT

Work in a group.
Make a list of different kinds of plastic objects that could be recycled to help the reefs.

Quiz

Choose the correct answers.

1 A coral is . . .
  a a flower.
  b a plant.
  c an animal.

2 Most coral reefs are in . . .
  a warm rivers.
  b warm and shallow water.
  c cold and shallow water.

3 A cuttlefish changes colour . . .
  a to catch food.
  b to stop big animals seeing it.
  c to catch food and to stop
      big animals seeing it.

4 What do dolphins do with coral?
  a play with it
  b eat it
  c watch it

5 Sea turtles go to the reef . . .
  a to eat small fish.
  b to find small plants and animals.
  c to clean their shells.

6 A bobbit worm has . . .
  a no mouth.
  b no teeth.
  c big teeth.

7 Some fish use the coral to . . .
  a open clams.
  b clean octopuses.
  c stay warm.

8 Plastic rubbish . . .
  a helps the coral reefs.
  b kills sea animals.
  c is food for sea animals.

Visit www.ladybirdeducation.co.uk for FREE DO YOU KNOW? teaching resources.

- video clips with simplified voiceover and subtitles
- video and comprehension activities
- class projects and lesson plans
- audio recording of every book
- digital version of every book
- full answer keys

To access video clips, audio tracks and digital books:

1 Go to **www.ladybirdeducation.co.uk**
2 Click "Unlock book"
3 Enter the code below

WILeOvb5CO

Stay safe online! Some of the DO YOU KNOW? activities ask children to do extra research online. Remember:

- ensure an adult is supervising;
- use established search engines such as Google or Kiddle;
- children should never share personal details, such as name, home or school address, telephone number or photos.